A LICK OF
SENSE
THE BOOK

Cowboy devotionals

PASTOR PAUL HOWIE &
DIXIE THE COWDOG

A LICK OF SENSE - THE BOOK
COWBOY DEVOTIONALS

iUniverse books may be ordered through booksellers or by contacting:

iUniverse
1663 Liberty Drive
Bloomington, IN 47403
www.iuniverse.com
1-800-Authors (1-800-288-4677)

Because of the dynamic nature of the Internet, any web addresses or links contained in this book may have changed since publication and may no longer be valid. The views expressed in this work are solely those of the author and do not necessarily reflect the views of the publisher, and the publisher hereby disclaims any responsibility for them.

Any people depicted in stock imagery provided by Thinkstock are models, and such images are being used for illustrative purposes only. Certain stock imagery © Thinkstock.

ISBN: 978-1-5320-0320-2 (sc)
ISBN: 978-1-5320-0340-0 (e)

Library of Congress Control Number: 2016911632

Print information available on the last page.

iUniverse rev. date: 08/09/2016

"A Lick of Sense" Cowboy wisdom, is a great gift for anyone you know who loves good old fashioned cowboy wisdom based in God's Word. Howie, pastor of Leon River Cowboy Church, has shared in small tidbits a down to earth approach to everyday life and following God's plan as we face issues from family and children, to livestock and the workaday world. I encourage you to get a copy for yourself and several for those friends and family that love the Western lifestyle, horses, cattle, the land and children.

Jeff Gore

In this new century, with so many people living in the city far from the food source, it seems that only God and another cowboy could truly understand who we are as keepers of the land and critters. Like the cows need grass and water, we too, are in need of nourishment. Pastor Paul Howie and Cathi Ball lead us directly to the feed trough with this collection of inspirational short stories suited for truth-hungry cowgirls and cowboys.

Tim O'Byrne

Editor

Working Ranch magazine

"To my Dad, Leslie Howie, who taught me to be a cowboy and my wife, Rhonda Howie, who taught me to see God everywhere I look. Through them, I found A Lick of Sense.".

In memory of Dixie "The Cowdog" 11/3/15

A Lick of Sense

"The Wisdom of a Cowboy"

A man's man ... no fear ... one who stares death in the face ... tough as nails ... the John Wayne kind of man. We lift weights, work with our hands, deny pain, all because that's what a real man does! Bull riders riding with a broken foot in a cast, workers doing their jobs with blisters on their hands, Dads protecting their families from midnight intruders. The real man ... six pack abs and biceps that bulge and no backing down to anything!

Or just maybe our idea of what a 'real' man looks like isn't *completely* accurate. The perfect example is Jesus. I don't recall Him lifting weights or taking karate lessons, but He certainly wasn't a sissy? He endured beatings of the Roman soldiers and the pain of the cross (with no pain killers Matt. 27:34), when at any time He could have called down 10,000 angels to rescue Him. He could have rode a bull in a cast and He could have thrown a bale of hay up on the top of the truck, but what really made Him a man was that He endured the pain for the right reason, not to show *Himself* strong, but rather to show the world the true love of the Father. Jesus didn't just endure pain, He did it with joy (Heb. 12:2). Now, there's a *real* man.

Now, if you'll excuse me, I have three more reps to do this morning ... John 19, John 20, John 21. Done. What a workout! I'm gonna be like Jesus one day (1 John 3:2).

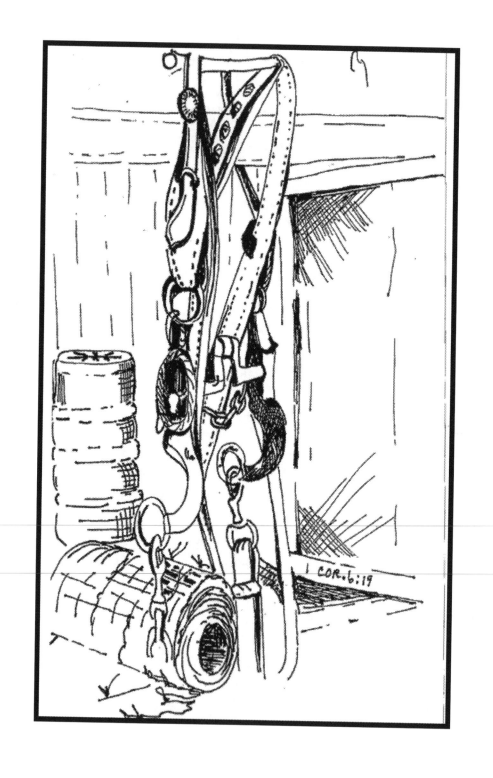

1 COR. 6:19

Call me strange, but I love to hang out in my barn. It's quiet and peaceful out there, and well, I just belong there. I'm pretty particular about my barn, too. I like to keep everything in its place; bridles hanging on their hooks, saddles on the saddle rack, buckets stacked in the corner. It's important to me to keep things in order, because rodents like to slip in and destroy things. If my tack just lies around on the ground, never being used, it would eventually rot away and the rats would chew it to bits. I'm just not gonna let that happen.

1 Cor. 6:19 says that our body is a temple of God. It's His place. It's where He likes to dwell. Don't you know it just aggravates Him to no end when we don't keep things in their place? Instead of forgiveness, we've pitched that out there on the ground and now the cows have trampled on it. And then t here's the love. It's supposed to hang on the hook close to our heart, but it's been dropped on the floor and the rats have shredded it to pieces. I won't even mention what we've done with the mercy. It must be in someone else's barn.

Oil the saddles and hang up the tack. Let's keep the barn in order. After all, that's where we spend most of our time.

A couple of years ago, just after we moved into our new house, I did a little landscaping to make the place look nice. I planted shrubs around the edge of the porch in a nice circular pattern to direct visitors to the front door. I was so proud of my work. It really looked good.

The next day, our puppy, Dixie, had dug up one of my plants. I scolded her and replanted the shrub, making sure to water it in good. Well, the plant didn't die, but it was stunted. It struggled to keep up with the other ones. Then, just when I thought it was growing well, Dixie dug it up again … the same one! So here I go again, giving it extra attention so that it doesn't die. It's a pitiful little plant compared to the others around it, but I think it will make it if I can keep Dixie away from it.

Jesus said that when the farmer planted his crops, some were choked out by weeds and others were burned up by the sun (Luke 8). I guess he didn't have a dog! But you know, there's always something that will try to hinder your spiritual growth. God wants us to grow to be like Him. He wants us to mature. But just when you think you're maturing in Christ, something comes along and tries to uproot you. Stand firm in your faith. Stand on the Rock of Jesus and drink the Living Water. And nothing can move you. And then, grow up!

Uh oh! I gotta go. Dixie! Leave that plant alone!

I helped some guys gather some cattle the other day. Some cows chose to fight and go against the direction we were herding them. Others just made their way down the trail without any problem. Some got mad while others seemed to be enjoying the drive. Some were fat and sassy and tried to run off at every opportunity. Others seemed sick and unable to make the trip. Some of the baby calves weren't mature enough to make it all the way, so they got to ride on the back of the truck.

When we got to where we were going, we had lost a few. Want to guess which ones we lost? No it wasn't the weak. No it wasn't even the sick ones. All the baby calves made it. The ones we lost were the crazy ones. They chose to survive on their own. That seems a little funny to me, because the only reason they were so fat and sassy in the first place is because the owner had fed them well.

I wonder if that doesn't describe us. Our Father takes care of every little detail of our life and all we want to do is fight Him, to do our own thing. The ones that admit their weakness and need for Him are the ones that are saved. He gives them that special attention.

I don't know about you, but I'm gonna ride on the truck with my Father!

I poured a concrete slab for the floor in my tack room last week. It is so great to get that done and now I'm enjoying it every day. The funny thing about the whole deal is how hard I stressed in getting ready to do it. "Man, pouring concrete is hard work," I exclaimed before I ever started! I put it off for weeks. Finally one day I decided, "This isn't ever gonna get done with me fretting over it. I'd better just grit my teeth and get to work." So I did. And you know what? It was hard work. But it was worth every minute. I can't walk through the barn now without admiring my work. Now I can enjoy it for a long time to come.

Maybe it's about time for you to jump in with both feet. Oh no, not in concrete … in faith! Maybe God has been leading you to obedience in Him for weeks and you've put Him off thinking, "It's too hard. I don't know if I can do this!" Even the disciples struggled with their walk with Christ. "It's too hard. It's tough to swallow" they murmured (John 6: 60). But the rewards of faith in Christ Jesus are incomparable. When you finally decide to take that step of faith and follow Him at all costs, you'll wonder why you ever waited so long.

What's God called you to do? And I guess the next question is, "Why haven't you already done it?" After all, He's already worked out all the details.

I love my horses. I try to take care of them as best I can. I buy good quality feed and coastal hay. I've built them a barn to protect them from the cold. I've done some great things for them just because I love them. And then … you know what happens? They're all fat and sassy and when I want to ride, they want to buck! They're not appreciative for all I do for them. You'd think they would love me back!

Hosea 13:6 says, *"When I fed them, they were satisfied; when they were satisfied, they became proud; then they forgot Me."* That's our God speaking of us. He's taken care of us. Just look around. He's given us everything we need and then some. And what do we do? We get all fat and sassy and forget about Him. We get to feeling so good that we start thinking we've done all this on our own and we don't need Him. Sometimes I wonder why He keeps feeding us.

Well, I know one thing for sure … I'm looking forward to that bucket of oats and I'm thankful! And if He wants to take me out for a ride, I'm OK with that. I'm just glad to be in His pasture. Oh look, here He comes now. Is that alfalfa? It is! **Wow. Isn't He great?!**

I got in a little late from the roping the other night. It was already dark when I pulled in to unload my horses and put my equipment away. Let me just begin by telling you, I have mice in my horse barn. Well, of course, I didn't have a light with me. As I was putting my saddles up, every time I would move something, a mouse would run out from under it. It was kind of an eerie feeling. I would have given an eye tooth for a flashlight!

There are pests in our world. They make a mess of things and do their best to destroy our lives. Life would be so much better if we could see these things before they build a nest in our lives. No, I'm not talking about mice now. It's sin that destroys our lives. It moves in and sets up shop. And left unattended, sin will make a mess of your life. If only we could see it coming. If only we had a Light.

Well, we do have a Light. God sent His Son into the world to be the Light unto men (John 1). He exposes sin. These pests won't chew on your life if the Light is shining on them!

There are a lot of great places in your county to worship. The Light shines for you if you will just give Him a chance. **Take your family to church Sunday and have a great day!**

You're in charge of a large spread. You rise early to make your rounds. The crisp air makes for a beautiful morning. However, when you get to the pasture, you find that the bulls have been fighting and have torn the fence down. Not the way you expected to find things. Several cows are out on the highway. One has been struck by a passing truck. Another has eaten some poisonous weeds on the roadside and is now sick. Stray calves have wandered into another pasture. How can this be? You've provided good pasture for your herd, the choicest grazing, top care, and security. Why can they not recognize how good they've got it?

Mmmmooooo. Yes, we're the cattle in this story. God has provided us with everything we need and more. I wonder if sometimes He looks down on us and wonders what we're thinking. If He looked into your pasture, will He find you where you're supposed to be, doing what you're supposed to do? *"I'm afraid that when I come I might not find you as I want you to be ... I fear that there may be quarreling, jealousy, outbursts of anger, factions, slander, gossip, arrogance and disorder"* (The apostle Paul in 2 Cor. 12:20).

Raise your head up for a moment. Look around you at all the green grass. Here comes the Lord now with a sack of cubes. You know, I think I'll just stay here with Him!

I heard a rodeo clown say one time, if you want to be a bull rider, all you have to do is fill your mouth with marbles and every time you get on a bull, spit out a marble. When you've lost all your marbles, you're a bull rider! Well, I think that's true. However, I do admire those guys' courage. But most all bull riders get hurt at one time or another. Nowadays, most cowboys wear a protective vest and many of them wear a helmet. Bull riding is most definitely a dangerous sport.

You know, life is a dangerous sport, too. Ephesians 6:16 tells us that our enemy, the devil, is constantly shooting flaming arrows at us. Like a bull chasing a cowboy across the arena, the devil desires to destroy you. So, put on your protective equipment (belt, boots, vest and helmet Eph. 6:10-18) and get ready for the extreme ride.

And, I didn't even know they had rodeo in the Apostle Paul's day.

Photo by

dudleydoright.com

A pretty nice rain we got the other day. I couldn't help but notice all the fertilizer trailers going everywhere just before the rain. It's important that our grass grows so that we have plenty of hay for the winter and grazing for the summer.

My teenage son works hard at growing. He eats everything in sight and makes those protein shakes. We went yesterday and got him a weight bench. Gotta pump iron, you know, and build those muscles.

We see the need for grass to grow, kids to grow, cattle to grow, our gardens to grow, etc, but we seem to overlook the importance of ourselves growing spiritually. Paul said in 1 Thess. 4:3 that it is God's will that we grow up spiritually. He's given us "everything we need for life" (2 Peter 1:3), but to be able to use those things, we have to grow in our knowledge of Him. Peter even goes on to say that if we do mature in Christ, we will be productive and effective (2 Peter 1:8). Pretty strong promises there, huh?

Yes, it's important to eat right, exercise, and take care of your body, but none of those things come with the promises of growing in your relationship with Christ.

Grow up and have a great day!

Last weekend when the cool front blew through, I went to put out some hay for the horses. Normally when they see me coming through the gate, they head for the barn. They know it's feeding time. But on this day, the cool air seemed to change their attitudes. I got out of the truck to open the gate, turned to get back in the truck and I heard what sounded like a train coming. I have no tracks on my place! I turned to see all four horses, with tails in the air, rushing the gate. I threw mud everywhere trying to hurry through the gate before they got there, but I wasn't quick enough. Out the gate they went. My wife thinks they've been plotting this for some time! I wonder sometimes why a little cool air causes them to change so drastically from their regular routine.

I pray the message of the cross and resurrection is a breath of fresh air for you. But more than anything, I pray that the message you received will break you away from your regular routine and encourage you to run for the gate. *"For the love of Christ compels us, because we are convinced that One died for all ... and those who live should no longer live for themselves, but for Him who died for them and was raised again." 2 Cor. 5:14-15*

So get out there and live boldly for the One that gave His life for you!

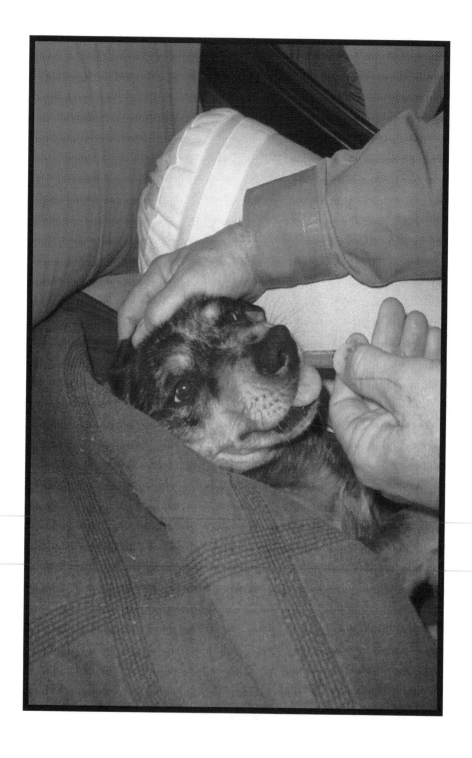

I spent all of last week sick as a wet puppy in a hail storm ... high fever, headaches, ear aches, no energy, you name it, I had it! Seems like I'm not the only one. Lots of people have been sick. There's definitely a bug in the air. Yes, I'm better now. Thanks for asking. I finally broke down and went to the doctor. The nurse gave me a shot (I'm not sure whatever happened to the good ol' shot in the arm). Anyway, I needed a weapon to combat this bug, and the doctor gave me an antibiotic. It seems to be working.

In this world we live, there are many, many impurities; things that damage us, things that confuse our thinking, and yes, things that make us sick. And anytime we come in contact with these impurities, we need a boost of the Pure. Where does a person get this boost? Living according to the Word (the Bible) Ps. 119:9 gives us a shot in the ... well, in the arm. David exclaimed that he would have died if he hadn't gotten that dose of antibiotics (Ps. 119:92). God's Word gives direction in all areas of our lives.

Been a little under the weather in life? Go to the Great Physician. Get your shots. And enjoy life!

When my youngest daughter was in preschool, one time they had a water line break which sent water gushing through the children's playroom. My daughter, always the quick one to supply the solution, shouted out to the teacher, **"Call my Daddy, he can fix it!"** Little did she know, I know nothing about plumbing! I'd probably have been running around screaming like all the preschoolers. But even though I wouldn't have been much help, she believed in me. She trusted that everything would be alright if I were there.

There's a lot that I don't know (understatement of the year), but my God knows all and I can trust Him. I live my life on the same principle of my little girl, "My Father can fix anything!" I know He loves me and would do anything in the world for me and there's nothing that He can't do. So I just trust Him with my life.

Near Jesus' last days on earth, He was beginning to feel the weight of the world on His shoulders and prayed, "Abba, Father, (Daddy) everything is possible for You." Jesus' model gives us comfort for living.

Now, if you'll excuse me, I think I hear my daughter calling.

Ever have a big cookout and invite all of your closest friends? Great times! Sitting around the fire, playing the guitar, singing songs, and cooking steaks on the open fire. But the real satisfaction is simply enjoying friends and family.

But what if you bought steaks, prepared the campsite, built the fire … got everything ready, and nobody came? Everybody had an excuse. "Well, I just got a new car and I want to go drive it around town." "I think I'll just spend the evening at home in my recliner." Now, you can't let those steaks go to waste. And what about all the hard work of preparing the campsite? Maybe there are others that might enjoy a cookout. "There are those out there that don't have much and would really enjoy my cookout." (Luke 14:21) God is preparing a great banquet (Luke 14:1). He's invited all of us. But the truth is, most people are too absorbed in themselves and not interested in God's banquet. But, as for ME, I'm packed and ready. I'm going to God's banquet.

I'll bet He's making S'mores,too!

Dixie dragged up a dead ... well, I'm not sure what it used to be ... something. In any case, it was dead and it really stank! She had been playing with this thing and rolling around with it and, well, she really stank, too. I looked at her and said, "You stupid dog!" And you know what she did? She wagged her tail and came running to me. "Hey, wait a minute. That wasn't a compliment. I said you were stupid."

You know, Dixie loves me no matter what I say to her. How much better off we'd be if we could all just love each other that way. But instead, someone does something that you don't like, you speak your mind about it, and ... ZAP ... another friendship is gone forever.

Jesus taught us to love people. He instructed us to love even our enemies (Matt 5:44). Paul taught that a person could have the gift of prophecy, great knowledge and wisdom, and even, strong faith, but if you don't have love, all those things are worthless (1 Cor. 13:2)!

So, even when someone smells really bad from doing really stupid things, the correct response is to love them.

(Another lesson from Pastor Dixie)

Love is patient …

love is kind … …

Jesus' birthday is approaching quickly. Years ago on Jesus' birthday, the wise men brought gifts. That doesn't surprise us. We always give gifts to the honored ones on their birthdays. And so, the wise men brought gifts of gold, frankincense and myrrh (very expensive gifts). They chose to honor the new born King. The reason we give gifts at birthday parties is to show respect and honor, but the gift reveals how much respect and honor.

So, for this Jesus' birthday, first of all you have to decide if you choose to honor Him. And if you do, what gift will you give Him? I was thinking about maybe a nice pocket knife. No, He already has a sword (Mat.10:34). Well, maybe a bottle of choice wine. No, He makes the best Himself (John 2:1-10). I know, maybe a warm sweater. No, that wouldn't do either. He clothes everything, even the lilies of the field (Mat.6:28). And if He gets a chill, He can just change the weather. Talk about a person that has everything (John 1:3)!

Yes, I'm just being silly, but seriously, what could we give Jesus this Christmas that would honor Him? Love. Give Him Love. Love Him with all that you are and love the people that He puts around you (Mat.22:37-38). Give love. There's nothing that would honor Him more. It's Jesus' favorite thing.

Good luck finding a box for that!

"Did to!" "Did not!" "He told me what you said."
"He doesn't know." "What about, you know, "the thing?""
"You're crazy! I don't know anything about "the thing.""
"Do too!" "Do not." "I'm outa here." "Fine." "Fine with me,
too." "Oh yea, it was fine with me first." "Augh!"

That conversation makes us chuckle, but we find
ourselves in that situation many times. It sounds childish,
because it is! We're so quick to accuse. Our accusations
lead us to arguments, strife, and anger. We take words out
of context. Relationships are many times severed because
of some of the silliest things. At what point do we realize
that our marriages, our friendships, and our partnerships
are worth more than that?

James left us with some really solid advice. *"Be quick
to listen, slow to speak, and **slow to become angry." (James
1:19)*** That short passage would save many relationships.
Listen to their side of the story before you speak. Understand
the situation. Remember that the person speaking is your
friend. **"Am not." "You are, too! Never mind**."

The Mesquite trees are budding and the horses are shedding. Those are sure signs that spring is here. And am I ready?!! We recognize the signs of spring around us, and we are immediately in a new frame of mind. We're ready to get outside and plant a garden, play ball, or just relax in the hammock.

Likewise, God shows us "His eternal power and divine nature" (Rom. 1:20) in His creation. And in the same way these signs around us remind us that our God is alive and well and still in control.

My oldest daughter came home from college last week. It was a beautiful spring day, so we decided to saddle up and go for a ride. As we were riding, I was aggravating her a little (that's what I do best!). I rubbed my hand across Tater's back and his shedding hair went everywhere. I thought the wind would blow it all over Lesslie, but instead a gust whipped it right back into my face. **"OK, Lord, I got it. You're still in control and I'm not."**

And boy, am I glad of that!

Looks like the wind is gonna blow today. Ever wonder where it starts? Is there a place somewhere up in the northwest that you could be in the wind and take one step to your right and be out of the wind? Of course, I'm being silly, but where does the wind start? Weathermen haven't offered any solutions. And when do you think the heating coil on the sun will finally need replacing? I mean, it's been heating the earth for several years now with no maintenance. And wouldn't it make sense that the closer you get to the sun, the hotter it would be? If so, why does snow fall from the sky?

You see, our God is constantly making Himself known through His creation (Rom 1:20) in ways that we can't explain away. I don't know why the sun doesn't burn up, or why snow falls from the sky, or even how the wind blows, but I know my God controls the knobs. All I have to do is trust Him. So when I'm working out in the field and a breeze blows through, I just thank the Lord for turning the fan on.

Maybe you're not trusting the Lord with your life, but you can't deny that He's there. **It's your choice.**

Last week I was working with some guys out on our property. As always, I had Dixie with me. Our crew had to make several trips to and from the property. I left my pickup there, along with Dixie (just wasn't a good place to take her). Each time we returned, Dixie was lying beside my truck. I guess she'd stay there forever until I came back. There's a lot we could learn about loyalty from a cow dog.

There was a time when many people were falling away from Jesus. Jesus asked the disciples, "Do you want to leave, too?" Peter was the one that quickly replied, "Lord, to whom shall we go?" (John 6:66-68) Peter realized that He couldn't leave Jesus, no matter how bleak things looked. He knew that the only hope was to stay with Jesus.

I hear lots of concerns about our failing economy. "What are we gonna do?" "How are we gonna make it?"

Well, do what you must, but I'll just wait by Jesus' truck!

I have four horses. Every time I pass by on the county road that goes by my horse pasture, they all pick their heads up with ears perked forward and stare at my truck. When I go to the barn, as soon as they see me, they come running. They are always ready to eat … always anxious for me to feed them. But when I want to ride and get a halter to catch them, they go to the other side of the pasture. I told them the other day (yes, I talk to them), "You guys are pathetic! You are only anxious to see me when I've got something for you, but when I need something from you, you're not available." Wouldn't that be a sad way to live? Life is only about ME!

Sad as it may be, that's the way most of us live, too. What can I get for me? How can I make life better for good ol' number one? Jesus taught a different mindset. He said to consider others better than yourself. Look out for their interests (Phil 2:3-4). James taught that if you humble yourself, He (God) will lift you. The way to contentment in this life isn't in getting more for yourself. It's in dong more for the people around you.

"OK Tater, we're going riding today and it's for your benefit!"

I went to the bank just the other day. I went in, made my deposit and went back out to my truck. When I got to my truck, I couldn't find my keys. I cupped my hands around my eyes and pressed against the window to see if I had left them in my pickup on the console. They weren't there. I checked both doors. Locked! I went back into the bank and retraced my steps. I looked all around and under the island where I had filled out my deposit slip. Not there. I'm sure the security personnel were alerted when I looked over the lady's shoulder now making her transaction at the booth where I had been. No keys. I can't get in to my truck. What am I going to do? What a helpless feeling. I had to call my wife and ask her to leave her job to come let me in my truck. But just before she got there, I felt something in my boot. Yes, laugh on! I had a hole in my pocket and my keys had fallen into my boot.

The Bible tells us that there will be a day when people will stand outside the gates of heaven knocking, trying to get in, but the doors will all be locked (Luke 13:24-25). Jesus will reply to their cries, "I don't know you or where you've come from." (Luke 13:27). What a terrible day that will be for many. You see, only those who know Jesus and live for Him will be allowed in. Wow. What will that feel like to be locked out?

I don't know about you, but I'm living for Jesus. I'm getting to know Him more every day, because He holds the key. Oh, by the way, while I'm still here, I think I'll go get me a spare key cut for my pickup!

I love to read the Bible. It's chalked full of events that lead us in life. But for me in my third grade mentality, I love to read these stories because they are fun.

For instance, do you remember the story when Peter was in prison? (Acts 12: 1-17) All his friends were praying passionately for his safety. Then they heard a knock at the door. "Oh, who could that be? We don't have the time for guests, we have got to pray." The knock continued. Someone told the servant girl to go get rid of them. She opened the door and it was Peter (God had miraculously released him from prison). She was so excited that she slammed the door in his face and ran to tell the others, leaving him outside on the porch. Well, they didn't believe her. "It can't be Peter. He's in jail. Please go away so we can pray for him." She insisted. Peter knocked again. Begrudgingly they went to the door and are astonished to see Peter. "Shhh" says Peter, "Don't alert the guards" (after he's been knocking for 20 minutes). They go inside and Peter tells them how God had made a way for his escape.

I love that story. You know what it tells me? It reminds me that God still answers prayers and the Bible is still fun to read!

Enjoy the Bible and enjoy life.

I went to Abilene over the weekend to a roping. Early in the day I noticed two little girls riding a horse out behind the arena. They were laughing and just having the time of their lives. Then later in the day I saw the same two girls crying. I found out their horse had just suddenly laid down and died. A vet on site said that the horse must have had a heart attack. One minute life is all great and in no time at all, everything has changed. I hurt for those little girls as they loaded their horse onto a truck to haul him off.

The fact is: All of life here on earth is uncertain. It can all change in a moment. James reminded us that we don't even know what will happen tomorrow (Jms. 4:14). So, why not trust your life to the One who *does* know about tomorrow? Maybe today is great. But tomorrow is uncertain. Give the reins to the Lord and rest knowing

He knows best!

I sometimes get up in the middle of the night and can't see, so I turn on the light. Our house came with all the modern conveniences. If I need light, there's a switch on the wall that does that. How wonderful was the man that came up with that idea? And then, when I want to wash my hands and face, I just turn a knob and water comes out. No running down to the creek with a bucket, the water comes in my house right when I need it. I'm praising God for the plumber that thought that up, too. We literally have all we need right at our finger tips.

Is it because man is so smart to come up with such great ideas? I don't think so! All of these ideas were from the heart of God. And they were all simply for our pleasure. He's the One that first created light by just speaking it into existence (Gen 1:3). He's the One that turned off the storm with no wall switch (Mark 4:39). He holds the keys to the storehouses of snow and rain (Job 38:22-30)). He controls the thermostat. And yes, it was our God that gave us these modern conveniences. Why? Well, just because He loves us (1 Tim. 6:17b). And He desires that we give Him glory for all He's done in our lives.

Look around you today. Splash some water on your face. Feel the breeze. Walk in the light without stumbling. And see how wonderful is our God!

Photo by Dudley Barker

dudleydoright.com

I love rodeo, even though some of the events seem crazy. Take steer wrestling, for instance, a guy gets off his horse while it's running wide open, onto a steer. Whose idea was that?! I wouldn't have wanted to be the first to try that one. At least in the bronc riding, they're trying to stay on the horse. But, on the other hand, if your horse was spooked and running off, it might be good to have a steer to get off on to break your fall. I guess it's just a matter of perspective. Ever feel like your life is gong way too fast? At some point you need to slow down, but can't find a place to get off. Well, you'll find rest with Jesus. "Come to Me, all you who are weary and burdened and I will give you rest" (Matt 11:28)

As steer wrestler friend of mine told me he'd never done anything that gave him more of a rush than getting down on a steer, but the rush just didn't last long enough. Sometimes that first move in trusting your life to the Lord is a little scary, but once you rest in Him, you'll find a peace like you've never known.

It's a little hard to describe … knowing Jesus. It's a peace in the middle of a storm, yet it's a rush that goes on forever. In steer wrestler slang,

"Get down, cowboy!"

I've got a great Dad! Even though we live 5 hours apart now, we talk on the phone almost every night. I have the utmost respect for my Dad. Growing up, I always knew when I had a problem my Dad would know what to do. And honestly, he probably didn't always have the answers, but I thought he did! And I believe that because of that respect, I never got in trouble because I didn't want to disappoint him. My faith in my Dad caused me to always be aware of my actions.

We should have the same respect for our Father in heaven. Is He really Lord of your life? If He is, your respect for Him should have a direct impact on what you do. Jesus once said, "Why do you call Me Lord, Lord and do not do what I say?" (Luke 6:46) "How can you say that I am the director of your life and yet you constantly ignore Me and do your own thing?" If Jesus is *really* Lord of your life, you will constantly seek to honor Him with your words and actions.

Of course, a whoopin' every now and then probably had a lot to do with my choices, too. But you know what? **I learned what a Father's love was supposed to look like. How about trusting God with your life and let Him show you what He can do (Luke 6:47).**

I remember as a young boy sitting at the table staring at a scoop of collard greens on my plate wondering what I was going to do with them. My Dad had already told me that I couldn't get up until I had eaten them. I really didn't want to sit at that table for the rest of my life. Now as an adult, I try to eat healthy, yet I notice that my skin is getting leathery and my hair is getting thin and my walk is turning to a limp. Maybe I should have eaten a double scoop of those collard greens.

The fact is, even those collard greens couldn't do the trick. Our bodies are decaying at a rapid pace. One day we'll all die, no matter how good we eat. Sorry for the bad news, but it's just a fact of life (or death).

But thank the Lord that's not the whole story. For those of us who have trusted our lives to Christ Jesus, even though our bodies are getting old, our spirits are getting stronger. *"Therefore we do not lose heart. Though outwardly we are wasting away, yet inwardly we are being renewed day by day." 2 Cor. 4:16*

I'm a child of the King. I'm not dependent upon this world. All of this will pass away, but not me. I'm getting stronger, and …

I ain't eatin' those greens!

People have been asking me what the New Year holds. Well, I don't know! But what I do know is that it's good. You know how I know that? I know it will be good, because they're all good. It's gonna be good because I serve a God that loves me more than anything and He looks out for me.

One time, Peter was thrown into a prison (Acts 12). King Herod had already killed James and was looking to kill another follower of Jesus. So Peter was in quite a situation. Maybe you'd think Peter would be really stressed out. But, no, that's not the case. That night, chained in between two armed guards in a dingy cell, Peter slept like a baby (Acts 12:6). Now how could he sleep? In the morning his head could be on a platter!

Peter was able to rest knowing that his life was in God's hands. Years later, Peter instructed the young believers, "Cast all your anxiety on Him, because He cares for you. (1Peter 5:7) There's a peace that the world can't understand that comes from knowing the Loving God (Phil. 4:7). Yes, it's gonna be a great year because my God has a plan for me.

I hope you're resting in Him!

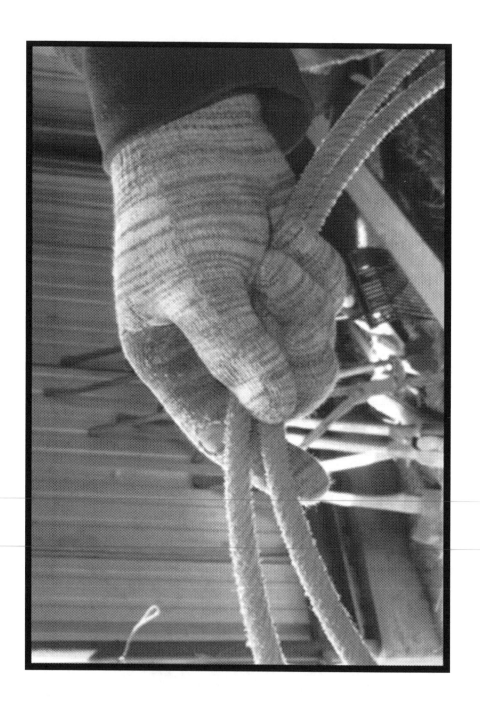

I went out to feed yesterday in this bitter cold. When I got back in, my ring finger on my right hand had lost all its color and it was completely numb. You see, several years ago I broke that finger, and I suppose it doesn't have good circulation even today.

Old injuries many times come back to cause us a lot of discomfort. Lies, deception and hurtful words have caused broken relationships that still cause pain today. But it doesn't have to be that way. Jesus recognized these old injuries in the Jews. Their eyes had become blinded and their hearts deadened (John 12:40). Their old injuries had made them numb!

The good news is you don't have to continue suffering with a numb finger. You can cover it with a glove ... a covering ... ... He covered our old injuries with His blood. "Having loved His own who were in the world, He now showed them the full extent of His love."(John 13:1b) Oh yes, it's still cold out there. And that cold can destroy you if you let it. But trusting your life to Jesus can warm you through and through.

As you celebrate this week, don't forget your gloves. And maybe you could give gloves to someone else!

May Jesus warm your hearts

Last week, my dog was after a frog under one of our shrubs in the front yard. She was determined to get that frog. She dug around and slashed at the bush to get the frog out. At one point, I called her name and she didn't even look up. She was focused on the task at hand. Well, in short, she destroyed my shrub, scratched her face up and still never got to the frog.

I wonder if that doesn't describe most people? We are so focused on making money and succeeding in this world that we don't realize the damage we're doing. In Jesus' own words, *"What good is it for a man to gain the whole world, and yet lose or forfeit his very self?"* (Luke 9:25) I mean, really, what good is all that stuff when this short life on earth is done. You certainly can't take it with you. All that work, digging and shaking bushes for what … a frog?! It's just a frog. It won't do you any good in the long run.

If you're gonna put forth such an effort, work at living for Jesus. He's the way to eternal life (John 14:6**).**

All frogs promise is warts!

We were riding back from penning some cows. It had been a really hot day with lots of *'episodes.'* The cattle were crazy and hard to pen, Tater lost a shoe and was a little gimpy, and we were all tired and ready to get home. As we were riding in, out of nowhere a cloud appeared, and with it an unseasonably cool breeze and fine mist of rain. It was soooo refreshing. All I could do was give thanks to my God. What a gift!

Last weekend, we spent all day at the rodeo. Dixie really had a full day. She played with the kids. She pushed the roping stock up the return alley. And she had to make sure Pedro was where he was supposed to be. She worked hard all day. As the rodeo concluded, the concession stand workers had dumped a cooler full of ice out on the ground. When I came by, Dixie was laying right in the middle of that ice. What were the odds that on a 100° day there would be a pile of ice on the ground?

When I saw Dixie on that ice, I knew exactly what she was thinking … "Our God sure does know how to give good gifts!" *"You know how to give good gifts to your children, how much more will your Father in Heaven give good gifts to those who ask Him!"*

I'm with you Dixie, God is awesome!

We're gearing up for hay season. I had a soil sample tested on my hay meadow. The results show a very low pH and low fertility. My land needs lots of time and fertilizer, which is gonna cost me a pretty penny. Also, the ground is packed tighter than my hat band on a cold morning ... needs aerating. And if that's not enough, there's weeds, lots of weeds!

Ranchers that are familiar with growing hay wouldn't expect quality hay to grow under those circumstances. My hay meadow needs some attention immediately!

We understand these things about hay, but why don't we understand these things about life? Luke 8 reminds us that the Word of God can't grow properly and produce a crop of faith if we don't spend some time preparing our hearts. Until we spend some time praying, reading the Bible, fellowshipping with other believers, singing songs of praise, and attending church regularly, then we should never expect to grow our faith. It amazes me how well weeds grow in poor soil.

I gotta get to work!

I have a lot of needs in my life. Don't get me wrong, I have a great life, but there are always things I need. All of us make additions to our lives to make them better: career, marriage, more education, cars and houses, and even hobbies and then, sometimes we still feel like it just isn't enough.

It's kind of like my hay meadow. I had a soil sample drawn a few weeks ago and it came back noting all the inadequacies in the soil. I added lots of lime and lots of fertilizer to get the soil back to a productive level. I followed the recommendations just as I'd been told. Now, that sounds all good, except that none of it will do any good if it doesn't rain. The rain is the key ingredient that makes it all work.

You know, I can add many, many things to my life in an attempt to make my life better, but the fact is this, none of those things work without Jesus. He's the Water of Life (John 4:13-14). Jesus *is* Life … abundant life (John 1:4, 10:10). He's the ingredient that makes everything else work.

It's clouding up outside. Yes, it's gonna be a great hay season!

Our recent fires reminded me of an incident a few years ago when the fires swept through the Carbon area. After the fire, I rode horseback with several other men to gather cattle scattered over the county. I remember riding up on a baby calf, left behind by his mom. She probably panicked when the fire got hot and left her own baby. I put the calf on my saddle and carried him to safety.

Jesus reminded us that He also goes after strays that have been left behind by the world. (Luke 15:1-7). When all is well on the ranch, you always have friends, but don't be mistaken, when the fire gets hot, you find out who your real friends are. Oh, I know people mean well, but some people just don't have what it takes to stand with you when things get tough. There's really only One that will drop everything to save you. He'll joyfully put you on His shoulders and take you home (Luke 15:5-6).

The owner of that calf was overjoyed to see his calf. He had lost many in the fire, but one was found!

I've been driving my pickup with the "check engine" light on. As a matter of fact, I've been ignoring that light for about 50,000 miles. I've learned that my truck runs just fine with the warning light on. Why should I worry with fixing anything? Yes, I see the warning, but I think I know better.

The Bible is instruction for us in life. It is useful for teaching, rebuking, correcting, and training in righteousness (2 Tim. 3:16). Many times, we see the instruction and understand it, but we ignore it because "everything seems to be going fine." "Why should I fix anything?" But then one day when everything falls apart, we realize that the warnings were real. God has given us a manual for life that will keep our lives in tune. But many people are ignoring the warning. The Bible tells us that a time will come when men will follow their own desires instead of the scriptures (2 Tim. 4:3). How many people do you know who are living life in spite of the warning lights? Any wise man will tell you that you need to get that fixed!

Oh, no! What's that knocking under the hood? If you see my truck on the side of the road, will you stop and pick me up?

I went to the dentist this morning. As I lay back in that chair, I couldn't help think about the last time I took Tater to the equine dentist. He tied his head up in the air, put this clamp inside his mouth and cranked it open wide and then took this big rasp and begin to file his teeth down smooth. I couldn't help but really be thankful that people dentists have more civil methods. And think about cattle, ranchers run them through a chute, slam their heads in between these two metal bars, squeeze the daylights out of them, and lay them over on their side. Yes, another reason to be thankful. I'm not real fond of going to the dentist, but this morning I found my appointment to be rather ... well ... full of thanksgiving.

Next week Is Thanksgiving week. You don't really have to look very far to see how much our God has blessed us. He "satisfies our desires with good things." (Psalm 103:5) Why would He treat us like a prince? Well, because we are children of the King! How great is that? So slow down a little, take time to see how great our God is, and "give thanks to the Lord for He is good, His love endures forever." (Psalm 106:1)

And if you can't think of anything to be thankful for, I'll ask my equine dentist if he has an opening for you next week.

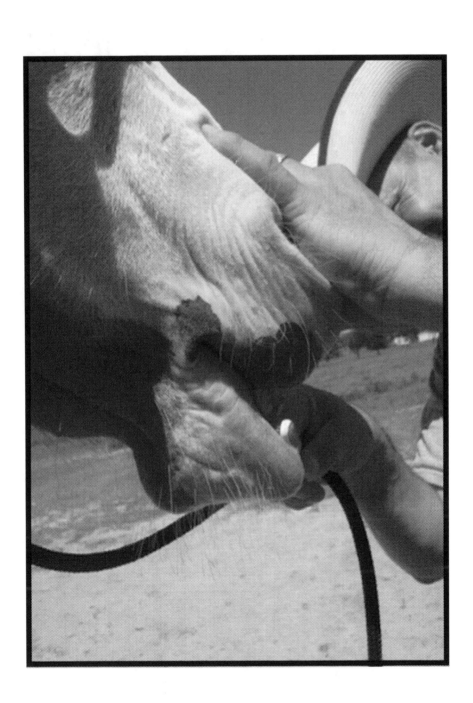

I try to take very good care of my horses. I hope they realize how much better off they are with me than out there on their own. I feed them quality feed and hay. I make sure they have cool, clear water to drink. I give them the necessary medical attention they need. And I provide them with shelter from the weather. You'd think they would really be gracious. But sometimes they seem to forget all that. They get fat and sassy and want to buck. That's a fine howdy-do!

I was reading in the Old Testament about a man named Jeshurun. The Bible says he "grew fat and kicked: filled with food, he became heavy and sleek. He abandoned the God who made him and rejected the Rock his Savior." Deut. 32:15, Jeshurun sounds like one of my horses. He took advantage of a good situation and got a little prideful. He eventually turned away from the God who gave him all of the blessings in life that he enjoyed.

I remember another man that got a little prideful. "I'll build bigger barns to store all my grain and goods: (Luke 12:18) He too forgot who provides for everything we need. Jesus reminded us that if we simply seek after Him, He'll give us everything we need. (Luke 12:31) God's given us all a great deal. Let's serve Him with our lives.

As far as the horses, I think I'll cut back a little on the protein!

Ever plant anything from seed? How is it possible that life can come from that dried up little seed? I'm glad the first person who decided to plant something didn't ask my opinion. I'd surely have told him he was crazy. "There's no life in that old seed! It's dead." But every year, farmers till the ground and plant rows of dead seeds. And in only a few short days, fresh green plants emerge, full of life.

As I sat down to write this article, I couldn't start until I found my glasses. My eyes just aren't as good as they used to be. Our bodies begin to deteriorate throughout the years. I'll bet I can get a witness! But the Apostle Paul said when we die, we experience life in a new body (1 Cor. 15:35-44)! From our old dried up bodies sprouts a new vivacious body that will never perish!

But there's a secret to planting the dead seed. There's many farmers right here in Eastland County that can tell you that the seed simply won't grow without rainfall. Water is essential for the seed to produce life. And so it is with us, without the Water of Life (John 4:10-14), there will never be life, the seed will just rot away.

So soak up the water, little seed and grow!

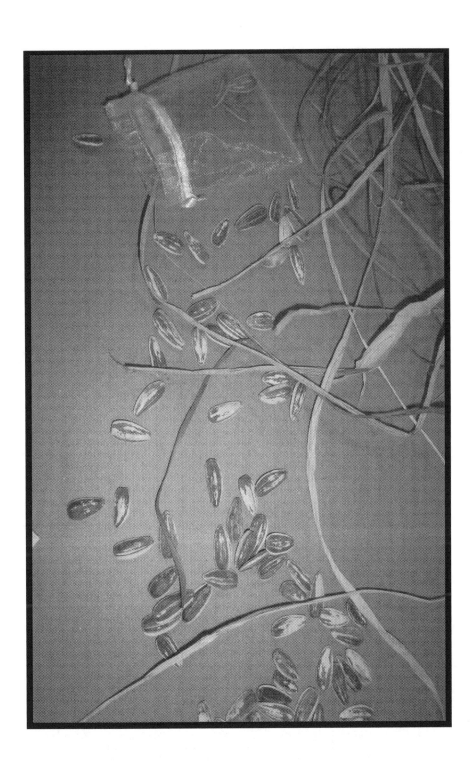

I had to feed the horses in the rain yesterday. I got my old Army slicker that hadn't been used in months out of the closet and headed to the barn. I could feel the rain beating against me as I walked across the pasture, yet I remained dry. Well, sort of dry. When I got back to the house, I noticed that from my knees down, I was soaked. Obviously, my slicker didn't cover everything.

David wrote "Blessed is he whose transgressions are forgiven, whose sins are covered" (Psalm 32:1). Are *all* sins covered, or is it kinda like my slicker? Maybe there are some sins that aren't covered. After all, we see unthinkable acts of evil on the news every night. And when David wrote this Psalm, he was referring to himself. What was his sin? He had an adulterous affair with his neighbor's wife and then had him killed to cover it all up. Now, really, how can God forgive such?

Well, He does. Jesus' sacrifice on the cross covers *all* sins! Paul said that the man who trusts God is credited as righteous (Rom 4:5).

Somebody needs to make a rain slicker like that!

At our arena where I grew up, my Dad used to turn calves out for me every evening to rope. I remember specifically one of those summer days. Dad had a piece of pipe that he would slide across the calf alley to keep the calves from backing out. The last time we had roped, he had leaned that pipe up against the fence. Unknown to both of us, the fire ants had built a nest up and around the end of that pipe. Well, on this particular day, Dad stood holding that pipe as he gave me instructions, "get your arm up, ride your horse aggressive, and hustle." While he was talking to me, the infantry of ants were moving into position. And all at once, attack! My dad threw that pipe and proceeded to do a dance that has to this day never been imitated. I watched in amazement as he pulled his jeans down right there in the middle of the arena, still swatting ants. I would have helped, but I couldn't get a breath from laughing.

I was reminded of those ants on my Dad as I read, "Put to death whatever belongs to your earthly nature." (Col. 3:5). Paul describes these as immorality, impurity, lust, evil desires and greed. They are killers and they will sneak into your life. And man, do they sting! They will eventually destroy you and your family if you don't kill them! One minute you're just enjoying life and before you know it, they're all over you.

We live with ants all around us. Watch closely for them and kill them before they consume you. Is that an ant crawling up your leg now?

I've always enjoyed the old westerns. There's always a good guy that goes into the saloon and confronts the bad guy. The bad guy always has about ten other dirty, unshaven scoundrels surrounding him. But you know the scene; the fight breaks out and the good guy whips them all. In the end, the good guy is standing tall, without a scratch, while all the others are lying around on the floor moaning and groaning. And while I really enjoy watching it, I know it can't be real. No one has that kind of strength ... or do they?

I was reading in the Bible this morning about Jonathon (1 Sam. 14:1-14). He and a young boy went into the enemy's camp and whipped some twenty men (v.14). How could that really happen? Well, Jonathon gained his strength from the Lord (vs. 8-10). Jonathon, like any of us, didn't have that kind of strength on his own. He trusted his life to his God. And the Lord is the source of our strength also. *"I can do everything through Him who gives me strength." Phil. 4:13*

John Wayne was a really tough guy in the movies, but that was all scripted. **In real life, the Duke trusted his life to the Lord!** Where do you find your strength?

I've been breaking a two year old colt. He seems to be scared of his own shadow. Really! He's scared of everything. I've spent a lot of time just getting him to trust me. He has to understand that I don't want to hurt him. I went to Wal-Mart and bought these big pink and purple balls. They're about 2 feet in diameter. When I work with him in the round pen, I kick the balls around. He's learning to ignore the big scary ball and listen to me. We have a long way to go, but I think we're making progress.

I know my colt is learning, but I'm not sure he's learning as much as me. Every time I kick that big pink ball it reminds me of something that God has kicked into my life. Leaving my family and friends and moving to Eastland, Texas was a big, scary, pink ball. Pastoring a church, a cowboy church, was a big scary ball, too. But you know, when I focused on God and His plan for my life, the big scary objects didn't seem to be a big deal anymore. What I realized (finally!) was that God controlled those things, so all I had to do was trust Him. Yielding to Him sure is easier!

Woops, there goes another ball. That one was even kind of funny.

My hay meadow looks as good as I have ever seen it. The grass is dark green and ankle deep from only cutting it two weeks ago. The horses stand looking over the fence, all glassy eyed and mouths watering. I can read their minds … "If only I could get just one bite!"

That's how we go through life. We see those that have better success than ourselves and we stand and look from the other side wishing we could have "just one bite."

What my horses don't know is that I have that hay meadow so that they can eat through the winter. And I feed them twice a day year round. They really have a good deal. They have no worries, because I am taking care of their every need. And that's the same situation we find ourselves in. God knows and takes care of our every need according to His glorious riches (Phil. 4:19).

If there are areas of your life that don't look so 'green,' just remember that it's the Living Water that makes things grow (John 4:14). He made it, He manages it, and He promises to take care of us. Oh, here He comes now! Is it time to eat again already? Isn't life with Him great!

Tater has shed off his winter coat and really looks good. For those of you that don't know, Tater is red roan. His red rust color with flakes of white really make him an eye-catcher. I remember when I got Tater several years ago, his color was what attracted me to him. I didn't know anything about him. All I knew was that he really looked good on the outside, so for that reason alone, I chose him.

But what I've learned over the years, it's not Tater's color that makes him a great horse. His gentle disposition, his athletic ability, and his willingness to do his job, make him a great horse. Those are all things that you simply can't know by looking at his outer appearance. You only get to know those things about him when you are with him for a long time.

It amazes me how we are so quick to form an opinion about someone simply based upon their appearance. The truth is we only get to know the truth about a person when we spend time with them. Only God can look at a person and see their heart. *"Man looks at the outward appearance, but the Lord looks at the heart."1 Sam. 16:7*

I'm learning to see people like God sees them; however, I still think people would be more attractive if they came in "red roan."

I'm feelin' a little tired today. It has been a long week. Ever just feel like doing nothin'? I suppose all of us get a little overwhelmed sometimes. I looked out at the horses this morning. All three of them were laid flat out on their sides. They were soaking up the sunshine and just enjoying a nice rest. I'd sure just like to sprawl out on the ground with them.

God wants us to work (Thess. 3:10), but He also expects us to rest. Even God Himself rested on the seventh day after creating the heavens and the earth (Gen. 2:2). And even more than that, God wants us to rest in Him, "Come to me, all of you who are weary and burdened, and I will give you rest." Matt11:28. And you've never known real peace until you've rested in the Lord. Everyday activities can sometimes be grueling, but when you've surrendered all of those tasks to the Lord, and you know He's seeing them through, then you can rest. He knows what's best for me. He's in complete control of everything that goes on in my life. I've given Him the reins of my life. So … I can just trust Him and **REST**

So, if you'll excuse me, I can't let the horses have all of that sun!

I bought my wife a glider for the front porch. Of course, it had to be assembled. Now, I'm not much of a handyman, and I really don't enjoy jobs like that. The instructions were very vague. I had to do a lot of guessing, which in turn, meant a lot of taking it back apart and trying another way. It was really frustrating! I was never so glad to finally get it put together.

Sometimes life can really be frustrating, too. But life is frustrating only because we try to do it without the instructions. "What instructions?" you ask. The Bible, of course. God didn't just leave us down here to figure it out on our own. He gave us a very precise manual. *"All scripture is God-breathed and is useful for teaching, rebuking, correcting and training in righteousness, so that the man of God may be thoroughly equipped for every good work."* *2 Tim. 3:16-17*

Those glider instructions were probably written by some guy in China who was working in a sweat shop for minimum wage. He was having a bad day and didn't care about me! But my life instructions were written by the God who created the universe and He cares very much about every aspect of my life.

I just wish He wrote glider instructions, too!

Living on a ranch requires a lot of work; baling hay, mending fence, feeding livestock, etc. But most of the work on the ranch is done without my attention. As a matter of fact, most of it is taken care of without me even thinking about it.

Psalm 104 reminds me of all the care God gives to the ranch even while I sleep. I didn't water the mountaintops. (v13). I didn't think about that! I didn't make the grass grow for the cattle (v14). I wasn't really sure how to do that. I didn't fill water troughs for the wild animals (vs.10-11). I almost didn't remember to fill the troughs for the horses!

"Man goes out to his work, to labor until evening. How many are Your works, O Lord!" Psalm 104: 23-24

As I was about to head to the house after a full day, Pedro (my donkey) sounded off a loud, "eeeeh- aawww!" I think he was saying, "It's a good thing God takes care of me, 'cause you forgot me again! (v10b)

I realize the ranch wouldn't operate without God. He's a pretty good hand!

When my kids were little, they frequently used the phrase, "I don't know." I'd catch them doing something they weren't supposed to do and confront them, to get in return, "I don't know." That seems to be a pretty popular answer even among adults. A felon is caught red handed in crime and asked by the prosecutor, "Were you at 555 West Apricot Street on May 29?" "I don't know." Yes, he does know where he was that night. He just doesn't want to make a commitment one way or the other in fear of what the next question might be. Kids also know. "But if I admit to this, what happens next?"

Who do you say Jesus is? What does your life say about Him? Do your words and actions cry out, "I don't know?" Once when Jesus was questioned about His authority, He questioned them about what they thought of His authority. Wanna guess what they said? "I don't know." (Matt. 21:27) Yes they knew. They just didn't want to make a commitment because if they admitted to Jesus' authority, their lives would have to change.

The Easter season quickly approaches and the question of the cross is put before us again, "Do you believe?" Why would someone NOT commit their lives to Jesus Christ? I really don't know!

Our society today teaches that you are successful if you work your way up the ladder to a job where you no longer have to labor, you only point and tell someone else what to do. But I sure am glad we have people out there doing the dirty work. Where would we be if everyone was promoted to supervisor? There would be no one out there to grown the crops that we eat. Not only would we not have the green beans and corn-on-the-cob, we wouldn't have the steak either. We'd be in a mess if there were no laborers. Yet, we are taught that you're of a higher status if you no longer have to work. What a crock!

The Bible says that the workers are of a higher status. (Did you ever notice that what the world teaches us is almost always different than what the Bible teaches? Ummm) In 1Thess.5:12, we are instructed to respect those who work hard among us! The Bible even goes on to say that they (the workers) are over us in the Lord! Our Lord views those who serve to the highest esteem, because they are much more like Him.

"The hardworking farmer should be the first to receive a share of the crops.: 2 Tim 2:6 To those who plow the fields, dig the ditches, raise the cattle, and carry the weight my hat is off to you!

A rancher can look across his herd of cattle and immediately pick out the calf that's a little sick. A cowboy can ride his horse across the pasture and feel when his horse has a tender foot. I see Dixie lying on the porch and just by the look in her eyes, I know when she doesn't feel good. How is that possible? These animals can't speak to tell us when they hurt, but we know. Why is it then that we can't see when God hurts? And what is it that does hurt Him?

Jesus said that the angels see God's face (Matthew 18:11). They see God's expression. And what do they see? They see hurt. They see disappointment. Maybe they even see a tear! What causes the hurt in God's eyes that the angels see? God hurts when we look down on those around us (Matt. 18:10).

God loves people. And it hurts Him when we don't love people. If you look around, I think you can see God hurt, too.

My hay stack is getting low. It used to reach the top of the barn. A person could look into my barn and say, "Now there's an impressive hay crop." But now it's mostly gone. As I was feeding yesterday, when I moved a bale, I noticed a critter had burrowed out a hole between two bales of hay. The hole was undetectable from the outside, but when I moved the hay, I noticed that much of the bale was gone. I would have never noticed it from the outside.

Paul reminded us to be aware of those that deceive us (Col. 2:8). People's ideas and philosophies can really sound enticing. But when you get to the center of them, you find that they are *"hollow and deceptive"* because those ideas are based on *"the principles of this world."* *"Fullness"* in life can only be found in Christ Jesus.

I hope your life hasn't been hollowed out by some critter, cause even though it may look good from the outside, it's bound to collapse eventually.

Out in front of my horse barn, there is a huge oak tree. I love that tree. It provides shade while I'm trimming my horses' feet. But it didn't get that way overnight. It was already a massive tree when I bought this land. There's no doubt that this tree was a twig long before any of us were even born. But over time, it became big and strong. And now that this big oak is mature; it has great value.

Anything good takes time. We always want what we want NOW. But the truth is, if it's not worth waiting on, it's not worth much. Did you know that God is perfecting you even as we speak (Phil. 1:6)? Through the circumstances that surround your day today, God is growing you strong and mature. I'm sure that oak tree grew strong through days of gentle rain and sunshine, as well as through high winds and hail. Some times are easier than others, but all of them are for your maturity.

Today I'm enjoying the shade of this great tree and thanking God that He grew it up. It would be of no use to me or anyone else if it stayed a little twig. I'd probably mow it down. **I'm also thanking God for growing ME**, because as a twig, I'm of no use to Him or any of you either.

Ugh! An acorn just dropped on my head! I guess God wants me get up and get to growing

I was riding Tater last week and noticed him a little gimpy. I got off and checked his feet, and sure enough, he had thrown a shoe. Now I'll surely get the shoe put back on when I get a chance, but for now, we've got work to do. "Tater, you're just gonna have to suck it up and go on." Well, it didn't exactly work out that way. Tater's a big ol' sissy. He was pathetic! The further we went, the worse he limped. Finally, I just had to get off of him. I didn't think being a little tender footed could shut us down? Boy, was I ever wrong!

In Ephesians 6, Paul checked off our supply list of all the things we'd need to do our job as Christians. Among those things were our breastplate, our word, and our helmet and our shield. All of those things are important. But the thing that really caught my attention was the shoes (v. 15). *Make sure your feet are fitted with the readiness of the gospel.* No matter where you go or what you do, you can't do your job if you're not shod with the gospel. The hope of Jesus Christ is all that keeps us going. Without Him, we turn into a bunch of sissies!

I had my hat. I had my chaps. I even had my rope. But with just one shoe missing, I couldn't make the catch. Sorry Tater, I'll be more ready next time.

Just got back from Oklahoma City where I roped at the National Finals of Team Roping. Wow. It was so much fun. I roped with my Dad. How great it is to share a time like that with someone you love. I saw lots of friends that I haven't seen for a while and even made new friends from all over the country. On the way home, I couldn't help thinking how God had blessed my trip. And then I remembered what He (Jesus) told Nathaniel. *"You believe because I told you I saw you under the fig tree. You shall see greater things than that."* (John 1:50) Nathaniel was amazed at what Jesus had done, but Jesus said there was even more to come!

I've been blessed in so many ways. But the most awesome thing about living for the Lord is that it just keeps getting better. So, you believe because you saw the beautiful sunrise this morning, or felt the cool breeze. Maybe God has blessed you with friends and family. Maybe it's … well, you fill in the blank. But whatever it is, God has more! *"He is able to do immeasurably more"* than you could ever dream up (Eph 3:20).

Kinda makes you hungry for tomorrow, doesn't it?

Love is not jealous ...
Love does not brag ... ...

People tell me my column in the newspaper is first grade "simple." I get asked, "Do you write these stories so simple so that people can understand?" Well, I mainly write them simple because *I* am simple. I never claimed to be a scholar. I just write what I know about life. And honestly, it doesn't take me long to tell you everything I know. But just because I don't know a lot of things doesn't mean that I want to stay there. I want to learn and understand the world around me. But most of all, I want to fully understand my God. All the wisdom I need is found in Him. So, I'm constantly trying to understand Him more. *"Therefore let us leave the elementary teachings about Christ and go on the maturity, not laying again the foundation of repentance from acts that lead to death, and faith in God."* (Heb. 6:1) No, I don't claim to be a scholar, but with God's help I'll grow up (Heb. 6:3). The comforting thing to me is that we don't have to be microbiologists to know the Living God. We just have to want to know Him.

Maybe sometimes I'll wow you with some big words ... but I probably won't know what they mean!

My kids and I have been watching the Ninja Warriors competitions. I'm amazed at some of the stuff they do. They jump from great heights to a rope and swing to another obstacle. They hold to a barrel rolling down a hill. They climb across cliffs with very little places to put their fingers. It wears me out to watch it on TV! Why would they put themselves through such turmoil? I suppose they just have something to prove to the world.

The Apostle Paul must have been a ninja warrior. Acts 9:24-25 says that *they kept close watch on the city gates in order to kill him. But his followers took him by night and lowered him in a basket through an opening in the wall.* I really can't see me hanging out the window in a basket knowing there are those watching for me in order to kill me! In a basket on a rope would make you kinda like a piñata!

But Paul, like a true ninja, certainly had something to prove to the world … that Jesus is Lord. Paul spoke boldly and fearlessly to advance the Kingdom. No obstacle was too big or too difficult to overcome. He was on a mission for the Mighty God.

Are you ready to jump?

As cowboys, we all have a story to tell. Maybe it was the cow that almost got away but you roped her just before she slipped into the thicket. Or maybe it was the time you barely outran a tornado in your old pickup truck. It might have even been the time your best friend ran the tractor off in the gully and you jacked it up to save his life. Man, those coffee shop stories are everywhere and we can't wait for a chance to tell 'em.

Jesus' followers all had stories to tell, too. Paul told of a blinding light and a voice from heaven that changed his life (Acts 9:3-5). Peter always loved to tell the story of how he walked on the water with Jesus (Matt. 14:28-30). And a little boy could tell all of his playground buddies how Jesus borrowed his sack lunch and used it to feed 5,000 men lunch one day (John 6:8-13).

Do you have a story? No, not a story about a cow or a pickup truck! Do you have a story about how Jesus has changed your life?

He's still creating stories in people all around you. I can't wait to hear about what He does for you!

Pedro is ridiculously funny! For those of you that don't know who Pedro is, he is my donkey. He's about three feet tall and his ears are about as long as his legs. But he thinks he's a race horse. He'll run full blast down the fence with the horses. I just laugh at him and shake my head. "You're not a race horse. Your ears are creating too much drag. You're a donkey." How could he think he's a race horse?

But you know, we're ridiculously funny sometimes, too. We get to thinking we're way more than we really are. "I can do this or I can do that." Really, you can't do anything on your own. You're not a race horse! Paul reminded us to think of ourselves with sober judgment (Rom. 12:3). So, here's the sober truth: Without God, you can't do anything (John 15:5), but with Him, you can do anything (Phil. 4:13). So, don't be a donkey! **Live a life of praise in thanksgiving to our Awesome God!**

I was driving home late last night. The weather was foggy and rainy, with limited vision. All at once I came upon an armadillo crossing the road. With no time to go around him, I tried to straddle him with the truck. And I would have been successful at sparing his life except that when I went over him, he jumped! Now why would he do such a dumb thing? Why not duck down and live?

I wondered why he decided to chance crossing the highway in the first place. Maybe life was really stressful on that side of the road. Maybe he'd made some mistakes over there and just had to get away. Maybe he didn't make a wise move to leave, but he still could have made it if he'd just NOT jumped!

We make not-so-smart decisions. It's not too late to make a good decision and live. Sure. life is hard. We make lots of mistakes and follow them up with dumb choices. But somewhere down the road, we've gotta stop fighting against everything that comes along. James said to "Submit yourselves to God." (James 4:7) So you made some mistakes.

"Come near to God and He will come near to you." (James 4:8)

Dixie and I walked upon a lake that had some ducks on it. Dixie jumped in and swam after them. Most of them flew to safety, but one duck seemed content to play with Dixie. The courageous duck swam just ahead of Dixie. When the pursuing duck herder would get closer, the duck would fly back over to the other side of the water. I just had to laugh at my silly dog. "You're never gonna catch that duck."

I wondered if God ever laughed at people chasing after things of the world. We work so hard to get something to later find that it didn't satisfy (Ecc. 5:10). Then we're off to the races again. We're swimming after ducks! And we're *not* gonna catch 'em. *"The world and its ways pass away, but the man who does the will of God lives forever."* 1 John 2:17 God has provided us with every-thing we need (1 Tim. 6:17).

You know, maybe we should have been just enjoying the swim all along.

Ever get so frustrated that you throw your hat on the ground and then stomp it? And then you realize what you just did, "Man, that was a good hat!" The fact is; sometimes life is just frustrating. The hay baler breaks down, the bull is out again, and the dog chewed the water hose in two! Aghhhh! Where is God in all this? "Come on, God, let up a little!" Is God trying to get my attention, or has He simply forgotten about me down here?

The apostle Paul found himself falsely accused and thrown in prison (Acts 16:16-40). Talk about frustrating circumstances! What'd he do? He sang praises to God. No, you didn't read it wrong. He really sang. How could he *sing* at a time like that? Paul knew God had a plan, and he knew God's plan was right (Isaiah 55:8).

Last summer a friend of mine and I were hauling some cattle. We had not one, but two, blowouts on the trailer. We inched along for miles while my friend told jokes! "How can you be so happy?" He replied, "God created this day for me, and it'll take way more than a flat tire to ruin it."

I hope Greer's Western Store has a sale on straw hats!

I wonder if any of our local ranchers ever sing to their cattle? No, I haven't lost my mind. On the old cattle drives, cowboys used to pull out the ol' guitar and sing to the cattle. It was believed that a song would calm the herd.

You know, we sing every Sunday morning before we study God's Word. Ever wonder why churches do that? Jesus once told a parable about a farmer preparing the soil for planting (Matthew 13). For the seeds to grow, the soil had to be softened up a little, and the rocks and thorn bushes removed. Jesus explained the story that the seed was the Word of God and the soil was men's hearts. Our hearts need to be prepared to receive the teaching of God's Word. So, … we sing. We sing songs to encourage us in our faith. We sing songs to calm our thinking of the brutal week we just finished. We sing songs to honor the One who makes all things right. Then, when the seed is sown, it can grow.

So just maybe there's more to a song than we think. If you're a little sad today, sing a song of praise. If you're feeling a little sorry for yourself, sing a song to the One who controls your life. But you know what? **I think I'd still feel a little silly singing to a herd of ol' cows!**

I get sooooo angry at Tater sometimes. I go to a roping and really want to win, but my horse is distracted by other things and doesn't work well. If he doesn't do his job, then I can't do mine. And I really don't think he's the least bit concerned if I win or not. He's just doing his own thing with no regard with what I'm doing. So, I lose again and drive all the way home thinking about getting a new horse!

I'll bet God feels the same way. I belong to Him (Rom. 7:4a). And, I have a job to do for Him (Rom. 7:4b). Honestly, sometimes I simply don't want to do my job. There are too many other things around to be doing. And so, how am I any different than Tater? Not much. I made a deal with God. I belong to Him. And what He needs me to do is *"bear fruit to God."* When I don't do my job, it makes it very difficult for Him to accomplish His work on earth. He chose to do His work through me and I'm more interested in doing my own thing. I hope He's not considering trading me in.

No, I'm not getting' rid of Tater. I'll just keep teaching him how important his job is. Maybe I'll come to a better understanding of my job, too.

I've always hauled my horses with the saddles on them. I guess I learned that from my Dad. Where I grew up, the barn was out back behind the house and a pretty good walk. When it was muddy a person couldn't drive out there. We hauled our horses home from a roping with the saddles on them so the horses could carry the saddles to the barn. Now days, my setup is kinda the same. I lead my horses to the barn and let them carry the saddles. I don't like to think of it as lazy, just smart.

We live in a time when life is stressful. I've never heard of more stressful situations; gas prices, layoffs, sicknesses, fires and drought. The load seems to be too heavy. Now I'm not promoting being lazy, but wouldn't it be nice if there was someone who could carry that load for us? Well, we're in luck. Jesus said, *"Come to Me, all you who are weary and burdened, and I will give you rest." Matt. 11:28* **There's no reason to carry all that by yourself. Jesus wants to help. Rely on Him. That's just smart.**

So when you see me drive by and you notice that Tater is wearing the saddle, just know that's not the only way I'm living smart.

I enjoy trading horses occasionally, but I'm always a little skeptical when I look at a horse that I don't know anything about. My first question is always, "Why do you want to sell him?" I figure the seller's response to that question will let me in on what's wrong with his horse. I mean, after all, the guy probably wouldn't want to sell him if he was perfect. My Dad used to say, "Every horse has a hole in him" ... which means every horse has something wrong with him. Lots of horses look really good at first, but when they get the rope around a foot or under their tail, they do their very best to buck you off. I'd really like to know that before I purchase one to make a roping horse.

I suppose people also have holes ... flaws ... something wrong with us that people can't see at first glance. Those holes seem to always come out when we get in a tight spot. We're pretty good at hiding our flaws, but we can be sure they're there. John said we all sin (Rom. 3:23). So, how do we protect ourselves when we're 'lookin' to buy? who to trust, who to be friends with? even who to marry? All have sin, yes, but many have been justified by faith in Jesus (Rom. 3:25-26). Those "holes" have been filled by Jesus.

Or, ... we could just ask, "What's wrong with you?!"

Do you brag? Most people don't like to admit they're braggers. But the truth is we brag. We're proud of things in our lives and we want people to know that maybe our life is a little better than theirs. I brag on Dixie. She is undoubtedly the smartest dog on the planet. I brag on Tater. He can really run fast. He's stout. And he's even the prettiest color, red roan. I even brag on Pedro, my donkey. I have to really dig deep to brag on him, but I can! He comes running to me when I call him.

I have an awesome life, therefore, I have a lot to brag about, but maybe I shouldn't think of it that way. Why should I brag? I really didn't have anything to do with any of it. I didn't make Dixie so smart, she came that way. I didn't give Tater his strength. I didn't even teach Pedro to come to me. He does that on his own (I promise ... I can't teach him anything!) Everything I have ... everything I am ... simply everything is because of Jesus. So if I brag, it's Jesus I brag on (2 Cor. 10:17). He's the Lord of Lords. That means, He is the best, greatest Lord of all the Lords that the world has ever known. He created all of life ... everything you and I know and experience (John 1:3). And you know what? He's my best friend! Oh yeah! We're tight. He goes everywhere with me. He gave me new life. Oh, sorry. Here I go bragging again. But this time, I have reason to brag. **He really IS the best!**

You know, I'm a pretty good shot with a rifle, too. Oops! I didn't do that either.

I got up early last Saturday to go to a roping. The sun was just peaking over the horizon and dew covered the ground. I walked to the barn to get Tater and whistled for him like I always do. He knew it wasn't feeding time, so he just stood there looking at me as if to say, *"I don't want to go today."* I walked across the pasture to catch him and he ran from me! He simply insisted that he not go to the roping. By the time I caught him, my feathers were really rustled. Tater's attitude was really aggravating to me. After all, I feed him and brush him and doctor him and make sure he has everything he needs. It's just common courtesy for him to serve me every once in a while. But, Oh no! He just wants to be lazy and stay home. Ingrate!

As I was chasing Tater across the pasture, I wondered what kind of lesson God had for me and sure enough, it hit me. God gives us everything we need and more. And what do we do to show our gratitude? *"I don't want to do that today."* Ingrate! Jesus once said, *"just as the Son of Man did not come to be served, but to serve"* Matthew 20:28 Jesus came to serve and that same service has to be our attitude.

It may seem like an odd time when He comes walking across the pasture, but when He comes, you be ready to serve. I promise, He'll feed when you get back.

I remember when our youngest daughter Cheryl was little, she always loved to ride. It was so cute to see this little, bitty girl up on Tater, who weighs in at 1200 pounds. We'd go to a rodeo and she'd ride all over the grounds like she owned the place. She was big up on Tater. She could see all around and get places faster in the crowds. But then she'd get tired of riding and climb down. I remember several times scolding her for getting off Tater by herself. You see, when she would get down, she'd be little again. When she was on the ground, she would get lost because she couldn't see over all the obstacles and she was vulnerable to get stepped on by another horse. I couldn't seem to get her to understand, "You're big and strong when you're on Tater."

But then, I guess I have a hard time remembering that lesson, too. When I'm with God, I'm strong. He gives me power to overcome. He protects me. He makes me big. *"Blessed are those whose strength is in You." Ps. 84:5* But many times I still try to go it alone, without Him. How dumb is that? I'll tell you like I used to tell Cheryl, "Go off by yourself and expect to get stepped on." Rather, *"Be strong in the Lord and in the power of His might." Eph. 6:10* Stay on top!

Next time I feel like getting' down, I'm just gonna step on my own toe!

One of my favorite pastimes is training horses. Some horses are so much fun to train because they want to learn. There's no greater satisfaction than when a young horse learns to stop, backup, or turn on his hocks at my command. I always reward the colt with a pat on the neck while he stands and rests. But then, there's the horse that just simply refuses to do anything I ask. He's determined to do it his own way contrary to anything I say or do. How aggravating that can be!

Do you know what God's favorite thing is? You and I are His #1 pastime. He loves walking and talking to you and me, but most of all, He loves teaching us to trust Him. He finds no greater pleasure than when His children are obedient to Him (Rom. 14:18). But, like horses, there are many people who have no desire to do what God desires. My Dad taught me about training horses. He used to say, "Make it easy for him to do the right thing and hard for him to do the wrong thing." And likewise, God gives everything we need to live in a manner that is pleasing to Him (Heb. 13:21). He makes it easy.

I love training horses. And you know what? I think I know exactly how God feels when I rebel against Him. I'm gonna listen to Him and try a little harder today to be like He wants me to be.

I went to a team roping yesterday. I was sitting on my horse at the end of the arena watching the roping. A team roped and I watched the heeler throw an absolutely terrible loop. It hit the ground out beside the steer and bounced and *accidently* snagged a leg. When he rode by me he said, "I had 'em both but that steer got a leg out." I barely could hold in my comments. "No you didn't. You never had both feet. You shouldn't have had even that one. That was a horrible loop." I refrained from speaking and only snickered inside. We often think more highly of ourselves. If that roper would have been watching someone else make the same run, he'd have been telling a different story. God wants us to look at ourselves realistically. *"For the grace given me I say to every one of you: Do not think of yourself more highly that you ought." (Rom. 12:3)*

Toward the end of the roping, I roped in the short round. A clean run would have won me the buckle. I roped the steer by both feet, but when I went to dally I lost a foot. As I rode out of the arena I commented to my header. "I had 'em both but that steer slipped one.**" At the exact moment I think I heard God snicker!**

I'm amazed sometimes at our prejudices. We think someone is better than someone else because he or she is taller or shorter. Who decided that? Cows are better if they're fatter and people are better if they're skinnier? A century ago skinny was sickly and plump was in fashion. And, wow, the color of our skin. White people think white is better and black people think black is better. And all the in betweens think their tone is best. Now really! Does an Angus steer really taste better than a Herford steer? I don't think we really understand our own prejudices. White skinned people go to the tanning booth (Solomon's girl thought she was unattractive because she was tan (SOS 1:6). Dark skinned people dye their hair blonde (and don't get me started on blondes).

Here's the fact: God loves people. That's it ... all of it. God loves people. All people (Psalm 66:8). Red, white, black, tan and orange (Are there really orange people?), short, tall, skinny and fat. He loves brown hair, red hair, black hair and no hair ... and yes, even blondes.

God loves people and thus, so should we. And we should love ourselves the way God made us. It's not what we look like that makes us better; it's Who we belong to!

I have a young mare that always seems to have her head through the fence every time I look out there. She's not hungry. There's plenty of grass in the horse pasture and I feed grain every evening. She's so fat, she grunts when she walks. But she just insists on eating through the fence and therefore, always keeps her mane rubbed out. I put cedar staves all around the horse pasture to correct this problem, but now she puts her head through the fence and gets stuck! She cut a pretty good gash in her ear trying to get back out.

Why would a horse simply insist on going outside the boundaries when I've gone out of my way to provide everything she needs within those boundaries? I guess that's a question we could answer for ourselves. Why do *we* insist on things that we know aren't good for us when God has provided us with everything we need? (Phil. 4:19)

Let's learn to enjoy all God has given us and be content with that! So, if I see you tomorrow with a big gash on your ear, I'll know you didn't read this!

It never fails, when we go to a roping, there's always some knucklehead who doesn't warm his horse up good and gets bucked off. Any cowboy knows you shouldn't get on your horse and just air him out, especially on these cold days. The horse will almost always buck. But to remedy the situation, all you have to do is loosen your horse up a little by long trotting a couple of rounds and then kick him into a short lope. Before long, he's loosened up and ready to go.

You know, people are a lot like horses in that same respect. Say you jump out of bed in the morning and hit the ground running, off to work or school. Well, you never got warmed up and the truth is, you sure might buck if you get the opportunity. By bucking, I mean resisting easy everyday tasks with a bad attitude. We snap at coworkers. We don't do what we know we should. We're generally unmotivated. Makes for a long day we brought upon ourselves. But what if we were 'warmed up' a little before we started those tasks? Jesus started every day with a little warm up for life. *"Very early in the morning, while it was still dark, Jesus got up, left the house and went off to a solitary place, where He prayed." John 1:35* Jesus always took time to get ready for the day. And the way He warmed up was to talk to God. **Everyday tasks can be stressful. You sure need to be warmed up good before taking them on. I'd sure hate to see you buck!**

I went shopping at a mall in Fort Worth a couple of weeks ago. You know, they call Fort Worth "Cowtown" but it sure doesn't seem that way. I was wearing my boots, jeans, and hat and, boy, did I stick out like a sore thumb. I wondered where all the cowboys were in Cowtown. As I sat outside the stores waiting for my wife to shop, I watched people walk by and glance over at me. I most definitely did not fit in.

Did you know the Bible teaches us to be different? Now, don't get me wrong, we're not called to be cowboys in the big city. But we *are* called to be "set apart" from the world (John 15:19, 17:17). A cowboy at the mall is really noticed by passersby as different, but most Christians living in the world seem to simply fit in. Maybe that's a good indication we're not doing the job God called us to do. The apostle Paul addressed his letter to the Romans identifying himself as *"set apart for God."* (Rom. 1:1) In other words, Paul did *not* fit in. I'll bet people looked at Paul just like they did me at the mall. But when others looked at Paul, they saw something different than they were used to seeing. They saw a man focused on God.

Do people do a double-take when they see you? Or do they just walk on by and not even notice that you're different? People always told me I was a little different. Well, now I feel good about it!

I got stopped on the highway by one of those black and white cars last week. Even though I do have a couple of speeding tickets on my resume' from the past, I try to follow the laws as much as I can. *"What did I do this time? I know I wasn't speeding."* The officer came to my passenger-side window and told me my license plate light on my horse trailer was not working. He was gracious and didn't give me a ticket.

Why is it that we get so uptight and even a little nervous when we see a patrol car? Did you know those guys are put in place by God Himself? *"The authorities that exist have been established by God."* Rom. 13:1b, God put authorities in place for our good, not to stand against us. So, the only reason we fear them is because *we* are not doing what we're supposed to be doing. *"For he is God's servant to do you good, but if you do wrong, be afraid."* Rom. 13:4

I really didn't have any intention of fixing that little insignificant light. It didn't mean anything to me. But now that I realize the officer who informed me of it was commissioned by my God- well, I think I better get it fixed. You know, I can't make claim that I am an obedient servant to God if I don't obey those He's put in authority.

Does anybody have an Ohm meter that I can borrow?

Man, what a day! I was sittin' around the fire laughing with friends, Dixie resting by my side, savoring the smell of steaks over the flame as Tater nickered in the background. Now that's life!

But you know, God said it'd be that way if we'd trust in Him. *"I (Jesus) have come that they may have life, and have it to the full." John 10:10b* When we look to Him for life, realizing that full life can only be found in Him, seems things just get sweeter! Think about it. We seem to think our own efforts make life better, but what part of anything you do makes life better without the Creator? Let's see, that steak over the flame … God gave us the cow for the steak. He also gave us the fire. He gave us plants to flavor up that steak, and He even gave us those little taste buds to help us thoroughly enjoy every bite. And people want to say, "I did that!" And then there's my friends, which also include Dixie and Tater. God gave us each other for companionship. What would life be like if we didn't have others to share that time (and steak) with?

Yeah, as I stretch back and chew on a toothpick and realize how great life is, all I can say is, "Lord, You really outdid Yourself tonight!"

I love spring. Warmer days and green grass excite me. All winter long, I've watched the horses stand bundled together with their heads stuck in a bale of hay. But here lately, they've been scattered all across the pasture picking at the tender, green sprouts popping up everywhere. I'll bet that green grass tastes like candy after eating ol' dry hay all season. And you know what, I didn't have to tell them to go out and graze. They noticed the green grass and went out to get it. They are enjoying life. You can tell, they have a little pep in their step.

I wonder why I can't be as smart as my horses. Green grass is popping up all around me and I've still got my head drooped as I choke down another bite of ol' dry hay. Sometimes I think God has to tell me, "Hey, Paul, look around. Life is wonderful." I suppose we all have days like that when we miss what God is doing for us. I guess that's why He has to <u>make</u> us lie down in green pastures (Psalm 23:2). He wants us to enjoy life. Because of God's love for us, His compassions are new everyday (Lam. 3:22-23). That's a fact. We just have to look around and notice His blessings.

I don't know about you, but I'm gettin' my head out of the bale because I see God's blessings popping up everywhere!

We recently had a playday for the kids at the Cowboy Church arena. The kids had a blast. Some of the kids could really ride well and then there were some who were just learning. But whatever level of rider they were, they all had a big time. I couldn't help notice Dixie. There wasn't a kid there that had more fun than Dixie. She loves kids. She made the rounds and greeted every kid there. She'd catch a small rock or a leaf or anything else they'd toss for her. She licked every one of them in the face that would bend down low enough. She even loved the snotty-nosed ones just as much as the clean faced ones!

I wonder if Dixie hasn't figured it out better than we have. Spectators would yell across the arena for a kid to go faster, turn sharper, sit up straight. Dixie didn't care. She just wanted to show the kids that she loved them. I do know one thing for sure. Jesus loves little children. And He loves them like Dixie with no regard for performance. He loves every child just because He wants to love them. When the disciples tried to turn the kids away from Jesus, He rebuked them saying, *"Let the little children come to Me."* (Luke 18:16) As a matter of fact, Jesus loves all of us no matter of how well we do anything.

Take a lesson from a cowdog. Enjoy life and don't feel like you have to impress people, because the God of the Heavens loves you no matter how well you perform.

Thanks again, Dixie.

Ever roped a crazy heifer just before she got in the thick brush? Yet, there was no steak on an open fire? But you ate it by yourself with no one to ooh and ahh with you. Have you ever won a ranch rodeo or a barrel race or a foot race, but none of your friends were there to celebrate with you? Sometimes we just need to tell someone about our accomplishments. But how do we tell people without bragging? As you know, God opposes the proud (James 4:6). I certainly don't want God standing against me, so I think I'll shy away from bragging about my accomplishments.

And then it hit me. Are those really *my* accomplishments? I mean, where did I get my abilities? Where did my strength come from? Who created the horse and the cow and the rope? I really didn't have much to do with any of that!

So the next time you feel the need to brag, brag with all your heart. Make sure everyone hears how great God is. ***"Let him who boasts boast in the Lord. For it is not the one who commends himself who is approved, but the one whom the Lord commends." 2 Cor. 10:17-18***

Man, that steak was good!

I used to read in the Bible how God's people would fall away from God and make idols to worship. How stupid was that. Remember the time Moses came down from the mountain and found God's people worshiping an idol they had made in the form of a calf (Exodus 32)? A calf! They were worshiping a statue of a calf, for crying out loud! Now I've seen some pretty good cattle. Ranchers put in a lot of work to raise quality cattle, and my hat is off to them. I like cattle as much as the next guy (especially on a plate). But I ain't gonna worship a cow, not even a live one! How ridiculous!

How easily do we also fall away from God and begin to worship ridiculous things. We sacrifice ourselves and our families to make more money. That's worship. We spend hours staring at the TV. Worship. We send our kids to camps to make them better at sports, music, dance, and who knows what else. More worship. None of which will last. Compared to the time we worship Jesus, well, there is no comparison. We've gone back to the image of a calf. The irony in it all is that God created all those things we worship.

Take a realistic look at your life. What do you worship? I really hope you're not worshiping a cow! That would be, well, ridiculous.

I went to the West Texas Fair and Rodeo last week. I always enjoy a good rodeo. During the bareback riding, there was a guy who came out really spurring. The bay horse was really bucking, but the cowboy was in perfect time and was making a great ride. Then all at once, cowboy and rigging both came loose, leaving the bewildered cowboy on the ground shaking his head. "You might want to check your equipment before you ride next time," I thought to myself.

Then I got up early Monday morning and went out on the porch to read my Bible, like I always do, and this is what I read, *"For the Lord is our Judge, the Lord is our Lawgiver, the Lord is our King; it is He who will save us." Isaiah 33:22* God is a mighty God. I understand that. I've got a great ride going. But the very next verse sent me for a loop. *"Your rigging hangs loose." Isaiah 33:23a* Our lives may be all good right now. But I certainly hope you've checked your equipment. At any moment your whole life could come apart. It's of extreme importance that we stay connected to the Lord; our Judge, our Lawgiver, and our King. Jesus left us with some critical advice for life, *"Remain in Me and I will remain in you." John 15:4 "I have told you this so that My joy may be in you and your joy may be complete." John 15:11*

Check your equipment. Stay connected to the Lord. And win the prize.

Cowboying has changed over the years. Nowadays, ranchers sound a siren mounted on their trucks to call the cows in. Maybe the rancher just needs to check to make sure all of his cattle are where they're supposed to be. Maybe he's checking to make sure none are sick. And maybe he's calling them in to feed them. In any case, when the siren sounds, it is for the good of the cattle that they come running.

God has called every one of us. Many have come running to answer that call, but many have stood out in the pasture and ignored the call. I simply don't understand that mindset. God wants to make sure you're not sick. He wants to make sure you're well fed. But most of all, He wants to make sure you're where you're supposed to be (we have a tendency to want to stray off). *"Each one should retain the place in life that the Lord has assigned to him and to which God has called him." 1 Cor. 7:17* Listen for God's call. Stay where He wants you to. You can trust Him for all your needs. He knows what's best for all of us.

I'm glad I heard His siren. If I hadn't, I guess I'd still be wandering in the woods.

Many of you farmers know the secret to a great garden ... poop! Yep, poop will really make things grow. A little cow manure will really grow some nice tomatoes. But poop growing isn't always good. I wouldn't have had to mow my lawn the whole month of August except for the septic tank. That poop really made the grass grow. The grass got so thick over the lateral lines that it would choke my lawn mower down!

And you know what? We've got poop in our lives and it also grows and will also choke us down. James warned that *"after desire has conceived, it gives birth to sin* (poop); *and sin, when it is full grown, gives birth to death (James 1:15).* Maybe it makes for bigger tomatoes, but it will sure make the weeds grow, too. We think we can enjoy a little manure on our lives, but it grows out of control and will eventually kill you (Rom. 7:5 & 11). And as if that's not enough, worms like poop. *"They worm their way into homes ... and are loaded down with sin and are swayed by all kinds of evil desires."* 2 Tim. 3:6

It seems a little weird that we're talking about wallowing in poop, but that's how it happens. You step in it the first time and go, "ewww!" But then after a while you're in up to your chin. **Wake up. Get out'a the sewer. Get back to God and let Him clean you up.**

It's almost deer season. I can't wait. I love to hunt. Cool morning air, full camo, shell in the chamber of my 270, not moving a muscle, I sit and wait. And then, I see some movement beyond the edge of the clearing. It's a buck. He is unsuspecting as he walks slowly grazing and looking around. Closer and closer he comes. Then a clear, broadside shot. Kapow!!! He never knew what hit him.

Now, hunting is fun, but it wouldn't be as much fun if I were the hunted. Can you imagine living life wondering if someone was around the next corner waiting to kill you? You know what, that's the truth of our situation. *"Your enemy the devil prowls around like a roaring lion looking for someone to devour." 1 Peter 5:8b* He's sitting quietly, waiting. Now, hunting doesn't sound like so much fun, does it? So, what does the hunted do to survive? You need a lookout. You gotta know someone has your back. Timothy had just that Someone. *"The Lord stood by my side and gave me strength ... And I was delivered from the lion's mouth. The Lord will rescue me from every evil attack and will bring me safely to His heavenly kingdom." 2 Tim. 4:17-18* I'd just say, make sure you don't go anywhere without the Lord.

I hope you get that trophy buck this year. I just hope you're not the trophy!

Love is not
jealous …
Love does
not brag …

Dixie has been limping for several weeks, so we went to see Dr. Billy Bob at the vet clinic. Now Dr. Billy Bob is a nice enough guy, but if it's all the same, Dixie would just rather not go see him anymore. To Dixie, *He's an underhanded scoundrel. First, he made me lie on my side on this cold table. Then he made me eat this awful gravy-like stuff. And on the second visit, he held me while another scoundrel held a mask over my nose. And when that was done, more terrible tasting something. Please don't make me go back there!*

What you and I know is Dr. Billy Bob wants the best for Dixie. The doctor does what is necessary for Dixie to get better and enjoy life. Sometimes those necessary times seem cruel and, well, very unnecessary! It might even *seem* like he doesn't like us at all. God promised we'd have trouble (John 16:33). Now how can a God who loves us so much allow us to have trouble? He should shield us from anything bad. Doesn't He like us? But, like Dixie, what we don't understand is these tough times help us to be stronger (James 1:2-3). It seems cruel at the time, but God knows it will make us better. Jesus said we would weep and mourn, but later that grief would turn to joy (John 1 6: 20).

And Dixie learned, *Dr. Billy Bob isn't really so bad after all. I'm starting to feel better already. Maybe things just aren't always as they first seem.* **Now we know that You know all things and we don't even need to question You. We'll just trust You from now on (John 16: 30).**

173

I was driving my truck down a county road yesterday, probably going too fast. In the road ahead of me was a dead squirrel and a big, fat buzzard having supper right in the middle of my lane. As I approached, I thought, "He's about to fly." I got closer and closer. "Now would be a good time to get out of the road." He refused to budge. I was almost to the dining bird, so I honked the horn. Again, he refused to fly away. "That squirrel must really be good!" At the last second, I swerved to miss the lazy buzzard. As I drove on past, I looked in my mirror. The buzzard still sat there eating as if he never saw my truck!

I wonder what would cause a buzzard to risk his life just for another bite. Why didn't he fly? Is anything really worth losing your life over? How about your career? Is your career worth risking your life? Has selfish ambition kept you from knowing real life? Jesus asked, *"What good will it be for a man if he gains the whole world, yet forfeits his soul?"* (Matt.16:26) Yet we just sit there filling our stomachs while death approaches (Phil. 3:19). Is that next bite really that important? The truck went around this time, **but you gotta know, not everybody is as nice a driver as me!**

Eastland county ranchers raise some of the best beef in the nation. And these guys work hard to do so. I hear them talking about the best kind of cattle, the best bulls, the best feed and the best methods of raising quality beef cattle. Raising the best requires dedication to the cause and a lot of hard work, but it's a worthy cause worth working toward.

I wonder how dedicated we are to raising the best *people*? God desires a breed of people who love and forgive. His favorite kind of people are those who live for the things of God rather than worldly treasures. So, is that the focus of our program? What are we feeding our children? Do we feed them humility or are we swelling them up with selfishness and pride (Luke 7:28). God has provided us with everything we need to raise a quality herd. And He's gonna hold us responsible for the crop we raise. *"From everyone who has been given much, much will be demanded; and from the one who has been entrusted with much, much more will be asked." Luke 12:28b*

What (or should I say, who) has God put you in charge of on this big 'ol ranch? Are you doing a good job with what He's given you? Or, does He need to find a new ranch hand? Sometimes I think if ranchers did the kind of job most of us Christians do, we'd be eating a lot more Spam!

John Wayne once said, *"Life is hard. It's harder if you're stupid."* Life *is* hard, whether you're stupid or not. And what is really hard is maneuvering through life and staying in line with the Lord. Actually, I'd say it's next thing to impossible. So, we all need a little encouragement.

I was trying to rope an ol' cow last week on Tater. I had just trimmed Tater's feet and he was a little sore. And as if that wasn't enough, I think he simply didn't feel like running hard. His attitude made my job really difficult. But I had my spurs on and "encouraged" him a little bit and we got the job done.

Like I said earlier, sometimes we and I need a little encouragement to live like God has called us to. Maybe we need a little gouge with the spurs. *"And let us consider how we may spur one another on toward love and good deeds." Hebrews 10:24* So, the next time you see a friend struggling with life, give him or her a little gig. Maybe someone you know has been rode a little hard or working on sore feet. Spur that person on. Encourage others to strive for perfection for our Lord. We need each other to get the job done.

"Ouch! I'm going. I'm going"

Photography—
Danny Deen

I was driving in the truck a couple nights ago. I pointed out the quarter moon shining brightly in the clear sky. I made a silly comment, like I'm accustomed to doing, "Look, there's God's thumbnail." I don't really remember where I heard that the first time, but all my life when I see a quarter moon, I remember being told when I was a boy "that's God's thumbnail." Well, without much hesitation, my daughter replied, "No Dad, God is much bigger than that." Wow! What wisdom. Obviously I didn't really think that was God's thumbnail, but I had lost sight of how big God is. He is so great that He clothes Himself with light as a garment. He stretches out the Heavens like a tent. He makes the clouds his chariot and rides on the wings of the wind. He set the foundations of the earth (from Psalm 104:1-5). Yes, He's bigger than our minds can comprehend!

So, next time you see a quarter moon, maybe you'll notice that it looks like a big thumbnail. But know this, God's a lot bigger than that! The moon is only a speck on the hand of the God who holds the entire universe together.

There's so much that we don't understand about our God. We can't fully comprehend His depth (Isaiah 55:9). But He constantly gives us hints of His magnitude so that we'll seek after Him. That's all He really wants from us and when we do seek Him, He's promised that we'll find Him (Jer. 29:13).

The recent rains have been very refreshing. When we see the rain coming down from the clouds, immediately we know the grass will soon green up and our newly planted seeds will sprout. We understand the ways of the earth, but many times we fail to comprehend the One who sent the rains. *"As the rains come down from heaven ... making it bud and flourish, so that it yields seed for the sower and bread for the eater, so is My Word that goes out from My mouth."* (Is. 55:10-11) God's word, like the rain, nourishes and gives life. And those who receive the Rain grow and mature and produce fruit. Drenched in God's Word, *"they will go out in joy and be led forth in peace."* (Is. 55:12)

The weatherman is giving a pretty good chance for rain today. I'm gonna pray that God rains all over you so that you'll sprout like never before.

Some local ranchers use a siren mounted on the truck to call the cattle in to feed. Over a period of time, cattle learn that when they hear the siren, they know it's time to eat and they come running. Cows recognize their need for the rancher. I'll bet the herd can't wait to hear that siren.

I wonder if we look forward to hearing from our Rancher (John 10). He's always there to lead us and feed us, but many times we don't come to feed. Seems like feeding time is only important if we don't have anything else to do at the moment. Sometimes it takes a serious tragedy in our lives to persuade us to come running to our God. A friend is injured in a car accident; we go running to God. A loved one is diagnosed with a serious disease. Seems a little ironic that the sirens are calling us in, too. It doesn't have to be that way. When we're listening to Him daily, we don't have to worry with tragedies. We can know that He's always there for us. *"When He has brought out all His own, He goes on ahead of them, and His sheep follow Him because they know His voice." John 10:4*

I don't know about you, but I'm not gonna wait 'til I hear the siren. I think I'll just stay close to the Lord and feed daily.

Paul Howie lives in Eastland, Texas with his wife and has three children and a grandson. "Pastor Paul" as he is known around the county, is pastor of the Leon River Cowboy Church in Eastland. Paul enjoys roping and is seen often at the arena with his infamous roping horse, Tater. And you never see Pastor Paul without his faithful sidekick, Dixie.

Artist Cathi Ball created this book and the images to go with Pastor Paul's articles which appear weekly in the Eastland Telegram. Cathi is a former Associate Professor of Art at Howard Payne University. She is married to Osage County rancher Chris Ball and they have three children. Also know as Mimi, Cathi has 6 grandchildren. Hound children include Maybel and Cannon Ball.

Artist—Cathi Ball

Artist note—I started to name this book **"God is an Artist, Jesus is a Cowboy"**.

The scripture tells us that if we "draw close to God he will draw close to us".

Jesus is coming back on a horse so he must be a cowboy … …

I welcome comments. cathiballart.com

C. Ball

Printed in the United States
By Bookmasters